Human —
God's Ineffable Name

Human —
God's Ineffable Name

Abraham Joshua Heschel

A New Rendering of
Der Shem Ham'forash—Mentsch by
Zalman M. Schachter-Shalomi

Albion
Andalus
Boulder, Colorado
2012

*"The old shall be renewed,
and the new shall be made holy."*
— Rabbi Avraham Yitzhak Kook

Albion-Andalus Inc.
P. O. Box 19852
Boulder, CO 80308
www.albionandalus.com

Design and composition by Albion-Andalus Inc.

Cover design by Sari Wisenthathal-Shore.

Cover photo of Abraham Joshua Heschel used by permission of Susannah Heschel.

Manufactured in the United States of America

ISBN-13: 978-0615652405
ISBN-10: 0615652409

*I asked for wonder
'Stead of comfort,
And yes, You gave me
Wonder.*

Contents

IV. BETWEEN ME AND THE WORLD

V. PANTOMIMES OF NATURE

Introduction

Anyone acquainted with the brilliant theological and philosophical writings of Abraham Joshua Heschel—with his use of metaphor, his evocative imagery, his deep wish to connect and relate, to heal and bring light to a suffering world—will find all of these themes and qualities presaged in his slim volume of Yiddish poetry, *Der Shem Ham'forash—Mentch*, published in Warsaw by Indsel Verlag in 1933. But I leave it to those interested in such matters to trace the development of these themes from his poetry, written in his youth, through his more mature theological writings. A translator ought not to write commentary for a poet. Any attempt to make the poet appear as if he had used a left-brained approach to writing his poetry is doomed from the start, as is any desire to make explicit all the varied connotations he wished to evoke for his readers. Had Heschel wished to do so, he would have written essays on the subject—though it may be that many of the topics he addressed in his later works actually do make explicit what is implicit in his poems.

Nevertheless, it must be understood that these poems were written before the Holocaust. A poem like "A Sunday in July in Berlin" could not have been written after the Holocaust. The Heschel who wrote *Who is Man?* and *Israel: An Echo of Eternity*, who frames the loss of Eastern Europe for us in *The Earth is the Lord's* was an older, more experienced and more mature man. Nevertheless, the identity of that young poet with the older philosopher, one of the great teachers of our time, is clearly evident. The young poet in love with life—feeling in all the chastity of his Hasidic upbringing and ideals the pain of his betrayed sister of the street, who asks God to let him help—was also to play a major part in the protests against U.S. involvement in Vietnam and the struggle for civil rights with Martin Luther King Jr. and the Berrigan brothers.

It is still amazing to think of how rapidly Heschel learned English after leaving Europe, becoming a master of the English language as much or even more than he was a master of German, Yiddish or Hebrew. Knowing this, it is interesting that he did not attempt English translations of his works on Kotzk (*Kotzk: In gerangel far emesdikayt*) or Torah as revelation (*Torah min ha'shamayim be'aspaklaryah shel ha'dorot*) as he did so beautifully for his work on the prophets (*Die Prophetie*). If he did not undertake the task of rendering these very personal poems into his own masterful English, how should I dare attempt it? I can offer nothing but this apologetic explanation.

When Heschel, whom I had known and loved for some years, suffered his heart attack in 1969, a friend, professor Edward Kaplan, borrowed the Yiddish originals of the poems from Heschel's wife, Sylvia, and sent me a photocopy. Overwhelmed by their poignant voice, their form and content, I knew that they must be translated. Even if only a small part of the original content could be rendered in English, I believed it would be worthwhile.

At first, I began to translate just a few of them as a simple get-well gift to cheer Heschel during his recovery; but the more I worked on them, the more I desired to translate the entire book.

When I had finished the first draft of a few poems, I personally placed them in the hands of my mentor with a trembling joy, as a humble gift from a devoted disciple. And, as he continued his convalescence, I would send him a few more as I finished them.

By March of 1971, I had completed a draft of all sixty-six poems and sent them to Heschel. His reaction to my translations was understandably ambivalent. I quote from a letter sent to me by Edward Kaplan:

> "Our rabbi was unsure of the value of the poems, as you noted in your letter, as he was dissatisfied with your translations. I cannot say to what extent, nor can I possibly judge them myself; Heschel was satisfied with some of them, but generally he was not happy, and had trouble writing you and telling you that directly. And as we know, he did not want you to circulate the originals. On the other hand, Sylvia Heschel reminded me that the tape recording you sent of your poetry readings, with the music, and the Yiddish and English, gave him great pleasure. He loved and respected you, and appreciated your sincerity and love; he realized the devotion you spent in the poems, and he did not want to hurt you; hence his indirect way of speaking in the letter which you quite properly characterized as ambivalent. Generally I would guess that he would have wanted to supervise a translation himself."

But as Heschel died the next year, I was never able to meet with him again to talk about how they should be revised.

In March of 1973, I wrote a postscript to the original preface I had put on the poems and had them printed up in a private edition which I gave to friends and students. It was an imperfect sigh of mourning. At the time, I wrote in the postscript: "I will not tamper with them anymore. At least Heschel knew them in this way. Were I to change them, I might move farther from his intent instead of closer." And thus they remained mostly unknown and entirely unchanged for more than forty years.

Occasionally, I would read one of the poems during a talk somewhere to honor Heschel, or to illustrate something, and someone would ask me about them; but still I had no plans to publish the poems. However, far from becoming less important to me over the years, I found that the poems became more important as I got older. I felt like something was left undone. In 2004, upon my retirement from Naropa University in Boulder, Colorado, I was asked to give a series of afternoon lectures on some of my favorite subjects. For one of those thirteen talks, I chose as my subject, "Heschel's Yiddish Poetry: New Translations," and I read from the translations I had made thirty-three years before and introduced Heschel the poet to a new audience.

Then, in 2010, when my student, Netanel Miles-Yépez, started his own publishing house, and it became a possibility to get out some of the lesser known works I had produced over the years, he asked me what work I was most interested in publishing. I answered without hesitation, "The Heschel poems." So we approached Heschel's wonderful daughter, Susie, whom I had known for many years, and asked her permission to publish the poems. She agreed wholeheartedly and we began to look at them anew.

Netanel, with whom I had been writing for years, believed that they needed some work before they were committed to print. But knowing that I didn't want to stray too far from what I had originally given to Heschel himself, proposed to do his own gentle revision that would preserve the alliteration that mirrored Heschel's own and most of the original renderings. Thus, he set about breaking the line structure of the poems for a more modern effect and making minor changes to words and phrases where necessary to serve the poetic intent in English. We then did a final revision together.

The final product looks quite different from the original translation and the original Yiddish, but is hopefully more accessible and congenial to the modern reader of sacred poetry. However, because of this, I do not claim to have actually 'translated' Heschel's poems. These are renditions *après Heschel*, a *Nachdichtung* of his poetry in English. I could in no way render all the rich connotations of the vast ethical and moral literature of Judaism in English as Heschel has done in Yiddish. Paraphrasing what he once wrote in *The Earth is the Lord's*, I want to say, 'even the landscape has become Jewish' in them. "Shrouded clouds" does not quite convey the sense of "clouds wrapped in *kittelakh*." "My songs hang before me like God's Holy Names" cannot render what Heschel means by "my songs hang before me like *shivitim*," a *prie-Dieu* image of God's Name facing the worshipper on the Eastern wall of the synagogue. Thus, in some places, I have simply left the Jewish words and images in the poem to speak for themselves, and elsewhere, I have removed them and tried to convey a good approximation. If they serve you in your spiritual or emotional life, or give some aesthetic pleasure, I will be pleased and hope that, in this way, I have completed my gift to my holy mentor, Abraham Joshua Heschel, of blessed memory.

Zalman M. Schachter-Shalomi
Boulder, Colorado, 2012

I.

HUMAN IS HOLY

I and You

Messages flow
From Your heart to mine,
Exchanging and blending
My pain with Yours;
Am I not You?
Are you not I?

My nerves' tendrils
Entwined with yours,
Your dreams meeting in mine;
Are we not one?
Embraced in multitudes?

In all others' form,
I see myself,
Perceiving,
In the laments
Of Humanity,
Distantly voiced,
Myself
Whimpering,
As if my face
Were behind millions
Of masks!

I live in
You and me;
Through Your lips
A word passes
From me
To myself;
Your eye's tear
Wells-up in mine.

In need,
Or distress,
Call me;
If You need
A friend,
Open the door
Between us:
You live in me
As in You.

Help!

Send me to
Death-bed-side
With a good word,
Some news of You;
If You cannot respond

I. Human is Holy

To that lonely call,
Send me to help,
Or someone else.

No righteous
Jeremiah's curse
Is my reply
To people
So poor,
So weak;
I think Yours
Is their guilt,
Yours their fault;
Their sin
Your crime,
Not theirs.

O God!
It is Your
Task to help,
But You keep still
Amidst human cries;
So help me
To help!
I'll fulfill
Your duty God;
Your debts
I'll pay.

Let me always
Feel and suffer,
When human hands,
In danger stretch
To reach the brakes
To stop Your world,
A brake You never
Installed.

Send me
To answer calls,
Like an eager aide,
To extinguish pain
With gentle help.

Send me
To pebble,
Rock or bloom,
To worm in agony,
Or to human being;
Help me to help!

For Yitzchak Levin, E"N

Millions of Eyes
Choke on One Tear

Millions of eyes
Choke on one tear,
Endless troubles—
Of entangled fates—
God, give me Your Sword
To sunder the Gordian knots
Brambling the Divine loom
Of everyone's destiny.

No, I do not wish
To bare Your fists;
I only beg of You,
Tell every virus—
"Thou shalt not kill!"
Forbid disasters
To run amok;
Banish the blood-thirst
From man and beast.

Hang me as a
Danger!-sign
Above the earth's
Volcanoes,

And set Yourself
As a sentry
Upon the pores
Of our flesh
That no disease
May enter it.

I bear the weight
Of all the damage
Caused by You;
Feel—I challenge You!
Like we, like me!
If not, I warn You,
I'll make the rounds
And scream,
For all to know,
That God forgot
His Heart
In me.

Suicides

An early evening star ignites,
Gaslights, a double row,
Like waxen deathbed tapers.

I. Human is Holy

Night, tell me!
Whose sighing lament
Does the wind carry to my ears,
Piercing all rest and hearts?

Somewhere
In the tormented chasm,
They gather bloodstained
Limbs and gore,
Suicide remains.

A heavy echo
Still hangs in the air,
A last and fatal scream—
I don't absolve you of my pain!

Obliviously,
We all serve God asleep,
But there are times
When through a window comes
Like from the guillotine a scream
Which wakes us, and asks:

"My thousand
Begging hands I stretched
To-ward you the multitudes
For help in dire need—
Why did you not respond?"

Human Eyes
Plead and Wait

Human eyes
Plead and wait
For help like a wick
That begs to be lit.

Humiliated brothers
Beg for help;
Betrayed sisters
Dream of hope.

And I promised,
Daring and bold,
To flood the world
With tenderness.

Yet still I trust that
I will span the world
With starlight in my eyes.

Forlorn

Lonely,
Forgotten by all,
Like a street lamp
Still aglow at dawn;
Unextinguished, unnoticed,
Flickering faintly at my door,
A humble heart beats to be let in—
Please! Open the door of your friendship!

In my love,
There is yet space enough,
And enough kind words,
To house you and your whole world
Embraced in my outstretched arms:
Come! Plant your gaze in me;.
Take up your dwelling in my care.

God's Tears

God's tears
Wet the cheeks
Of the outcast

And shamed;
How I want to
Wipe those tears!

If there be one
In whose veins
Trembles a silent shudder
Wrought by God,
Let them touch their lips
To the very toenail of the poor.

To the worm crushed
Under careless heel,
God calls—"My Holy Martyr!"
Far fairer is the sin of the poor
Than the good-works of the rich.

God and Human

Sacrifice
You ask not
For Your Self,
But to gentle those
Betrayed by Your love;
Have pity Lord,
Not for glory's sake,

But for those forsaken
By their own.

Blasphemy
Does not offend You
More than cries of pain
And human tears;
To You, no heresy
Is more obscene
Than deeds that cause
Human despair.

The one who stains
This sacred world—
It is You, Most High,
Whom they shame;
To serve with love
Your people, Lord,
Such caring work
Your Name sustains.

Battle and Victory

Don't give me weapons as a gift,
Or a victor's flush of glory;
I don't want to win, to prevail—
All this combat is my loss.

Grant me heroic constancy in love,
A caring heart, feeling without bounds,
To offer a limitless friendship,
Forbearing without end.

Grant me senses,
Strong and bright,
To give joy and help;
May I feel the urgent throb—
The call of every human being.

From One Heart To Another

How small
The distance
From my heart
To yours!
My own stirrings
And desires
I know so well—
How can I still be
So blind to yours?

A million eyes search
For but one contact—

I. Human is Holy

Like hungry spiders,
Each avoids the other,
Blinded to love,
Devoid of trust.

Let me confess to you
My own heart's longing,
And, bridging the countless
Lands separating us,
Become, my Self, at last,
The way to reach you.

Night Lament

Drowsy,
Tired houses
Squat in torpor,
Silent sufferers
Stirring in them;
A shard of life
On a threadbare quilt
Winks to a trick,
Promising lust's joys
For a buck or two;
People loiter, laugh,
Saying, "Alright!"

Cars bark,
Bark—"hark!"
Rolling trolleys
Rolling, lolling;
Bedlams issue
Pitiable pleas—
"Will our hope's
Pregnant seeds
Ever grow to fruit?
Will they rot?"

Sidewalk corpses
Lie embalmed in snow,
Like a poor whore—
The river shivers;
Heavens weep
In my bosom,
A sinister
Sinking woe;
Winds wail
And weep—
"Help!"
As if, in me,
God were at hand!
Why do You not
Help You!?

I. Human is Holy

I hear
My body tick
Like some
Insomniac's clock,
Through dinky,
Dying streets,
Furtive footsteps
Making their way,
While streetlights thread
Rays of yearning
Through tired,
Sleepy needles' eyes.

My booze-stoned brother
Rocks like a soft candle
Held in a sweaty palm
And taps a feverish tattoo
On the cobbled walk,
As if guiding
Geese to the slaughter;
Or does he yearn for me,
For home, or human love?
He would, these failing him,
Light his butt by the streetlamp
And rasp a tune,
"Lady Night,
Retched me up,
To rebuke me,

Puke-by-puke;
Like flies abuzz,
Fly the lying lies;
Like a comatose sufferer
The world is sunk in muted sleep;
Somewhere in the dark
Someone's pain leaps up
In an agonized scream;
A poet-mystic in wailing prayer
Hears a weeping—
Luminous of God.

Written in 1929

II.
BEARING WITNESS

God Pursues Me Everywhere

God pursues me
Everywhere,
Enmeshes me
In glances,
And blinds
My sightless back
Like flaming sun.

God,
Like a forest dense,
Pursues me;
My lips are tender,
Mute and amazed,
Like a child lost
In an ancient
And sacred grove.

God pursues me
Like a silent shudder;
I wish for tranquility and rest—
But God urges: Come!
And see, how visions
Walk like the homeless
On the streets.

Human — God's Ineffable Name

My thoughts walk about
Like a vagrant mystery—
Walking through the
World's long corridor;
At times, I see
God's featureless face
Hovering over me.

God pursues me
In the streetcars and cafes,
Every shining apple
Is my crystal sphere
To see how mysteries are born
And visions come to be.

Dedicated to my teacher
David Koigan, of blessed memory.

The Word Most Precious

Each moment
Greets my life,
A message clear
From timelessness;
All names and words
Recall to me the word
Most precious—*God!*

Pebbles twinkle like stars,
Silent raindrops echo true
What all creation echoes,
My Parent, Teacher,
A word from You!

My All, Your Name
Is my refuge!
Without Your nearness
I am nothing,
Lonely and saddened
By the thought.

All I possess,
Is this word—
If forgetfulness
Would steal a name from me,
Let it be mine and not Yours,
Screams my heart in dread.

My every word
Becomes a nickname for You,
"Woods" and "Night,"
"Ah" and "Yes"—
With all my moments
Weaving sacred time,
A bit of ever and always
As my gift to You.

Would that for Eternity
I could celebrate
A holiday of You;
Not just a day—
A *lifetime, please!*
How insignificant
My thrift and gifts.

Of offerings and adoration,
What can my efforts do,
But to wander everywhere
And bear living witness
To my caring?

Need

Silently, like a growing hair,
A feeling, deep down, moves in me,
A feeling of truth that feels for you!

Feelings alarm us,
To give them word,
To make them heard;
Where can I find traces
Of Your scent?
I fear the threat

Of unnamed longings,
Feelings cramped in narrow spaces;
I choke on what I don't know.

Save me, holy word!
God, I call You—Hey there!
Hey! Hey!

I'll disappear
Through night,
Past stars and trees;
Hey! in silence,
Scream and call—
Hey! Hey!
Silently, like a growing hair,
A fire is fanned, my soul a'glow,
Though why and where,
I do not know.

Brother God

God, confined,
Straight-jacketed
In labyrinths of the Infinite,
Afoot on sidewalks, fleeting,
Oh! How divinity masks You God!

Almighty is not your only attribute;
You are sad and bitter too;
Sometimes You treat me,
Like a child treats its elders,
With awe.

Our Brother,
Which art in Heaven,
At the endlessness, final light,
Tender down to us and gently kiss
Each creature with soft embrace.

Promise

My smile,
I feel to be your crown,
And my delight
Your fortune;
If I suffer some
Insignificant need,
Your pain for me
Is infinite.

My melancholy
Hurts You so;
How I ought to make

A holy revel,
Intoxicated
By your name!
To be the wick for
Your holy flame!

God!
With all my strength
I promise You—
I'll hide my sorrow
From my self;
On no account
Must my bloody pain
Stain You with my sadness.

Intimate Hymn

From word
To word I roam,
From dawn to dusk;
Dream in, dream out—
I pass myself
And towns,
A human satellite.

I wait,
Hopeful,
As one who waits
At the rock
For the spring
To well forth
And well on;
I feel bright
As if tented
In the Milky Way;
To urge the world to feel
I walk through
Lonesome solitudes.

All around me
Lightening explodes
Sparks from my glance,
To reveal all light,
To unveil faces
Everywhere;
God-ward,
Onward to the
Final weighing,
Overcoming heavy
Weight with thirst;
Constantly,
The longings of all
Born, call out,

"Is anyone there?"
I know each one is
God—but in my heart
There struggles a tear;
When of people
And rocks and trees I hear,
Pleading, "Feel us!"
Begging, "See us!"
God! Lend me your eyes!

I came to be,
To sow the seed of
Sight in the world,
To unmask the God
Who is disguised as world—
And yes, I wait to be
The first to announce
"The Dawn."

For H.N. Bialik

At Dusk

I

Houses, hovering mists of stone,
Trees, tracing thousands of arms,

Archetypes 'roused again.
Earth dreams blindly
Of the Cosmic wound;
Wind, storming silence,
Dares to break open
God's lock and wonder . . .

To breach a space
In the wall of time;
In the meanwhile,
Despair grows;
Who will soothe
The whole world's woes?

For every tick,
Every splinter of time,
On the clock of my joy
Eternity echoes, tock.

II

Houses, hovering mists of stone,
Trees, tracing thousands of arms,
Archetypes 'roused again.

I am your
Hostage
To the world;
How can I pay

II. Bearing Witness

The debits
On my name
With my own
Displaced fate
In pawn?

No dream
Can penetrate
The world
When my home
Is nowhere
In the line
Of sight,
Except on
The inside
Of my eyes.

Still I hear
My own soul
Swear her oath
By the God
Who is no
Happenstance;
So too
My life is not
Due to chance.

III

Houses, hovering mists of stone,
Trees, tracing thousands of arms,
Archetypes 'roused again.
Every face
Is a life buoy
In the dark pond
Of loneliness
We grasp to keep
From drowning.

Before the fiat,
You made longing;
After that,
Earth and Heaven;
Yet our home
Is not yet built.

Too distant
Even the most
Intimate;
Space breaks
And enters
Cosmos' bounds,
Opens gates
To reach
Far and wide.

IV

I am
A trace of You
In the world,
And every being
Is an entrance;
May I trace
Each outline clear,
And through all things
Come close to you.

Palaces in Time

Evenings,
Palaces in Time.

You,
My God,
Dwell in them
Richly;
Please,
Let my longing
Reside in them
Too,
To glean
The wonders

Of each nook,
And serve
Your treasures
To a world
In need.
Evenings,
Palaces in Time.

City Evenings

Somewhere,
In Heaven,
A film is shown
Projecting pictures
Past the stars—
City evenings.

Houses,
Immobile
As captives
In a mirror—
Not made
Of solid brick,
But diffracted light,
We run relays
From God's face;

Harnessed in
Reins of rays.

Our faces
Are but fragments
Of that very God;
Every glance
Is some secret
Disclosed;
All words
Dream of passion—
An echo of Divine
Compassion.

On streets paved
With precious gems,
The light lies tired
From a long journey;
O Beauty of
Transcendent space!
Senses brighter than
The brightest dream!

Trees are doorposts
Standing guard
At homes to which
We dare not stare;
With longing eyes

I stand at the gate
And beg for wonders
From God's rich estate.

Suddenly,
A shudder bursts
Like a command;
Urgency grips my
Heart and soul,
Bids me read
Between the
Lines of persons,
To enter homes
Past night-barred doors;
Then the senses fail
To feel it all.

Berlin

Street Dusk

Space
Is not filled
With air
But with
Unseen light.

II. Bearing Witness

Lamps suspended
In their center
Reveal frozen light!
The pavement's
Flannel blanket
Covers keyboards
Of alien scales,
Emitting sounds
That mute and hush;
And I pursue
Their heady scent.

Oh that I may
As first of others
Yet to come
Pray here
And join your
Choral sound!

In thrall,
I seek my way
Among you,
As one lost
In some sacred maze;
I hear a sound
Of whispers mixed
With screamed desires,
Or perhaps

The prayer murmur
Of unassembled choirs
Clamoring for the graces
Of an unknown God,
Or those of a great
Non-Self.
Oh that I may
As first of others
Yet to come
Pray here
And join your
Choral sound!

Streets!

Hymn to the Lord of Time
At the Very Last Hour

Each hour's fascination
Beckons to my desire—
Like some curious,
Eager, adolescent timepiece
Thirsting for evermore.

And every evening passes,
Heavy, like a train departing

II. Bearing Witness

With my beloved aboard,
Exacting years of dream
From me.

The narrow ridge
Of Life's last night,
When Lord of time
I'll give you the
Sweet remainder
Of my life,

How fully then
My heart will
Offer to You,
Your treasure
And bid You
A good Eternity
For evermore!

III.

TO A WOMAN IN A DREAM

To a Woman in a Dream

Grant me
A breath,
A finger's touch
In 'change
For countless hours
Of yearning;
Please say
Just one kind word!

All my young years
I dreamed of you;
My youth was
Sundered from you;
My dream
Hurt so deeply;
My great desire
I owe to you;
I beg you to
Save that dream!

Your eyes are
A message from God,
Your body my spring
In a desert expanse;
Pure joy you are

For my homeless eyes,
Your thighs beckon
Like sensuous trees.
In the garden of
Tiptoed quickening.

In dream filled nights
I sought you out;
Yet never did you come
To soothe desires
Not to be extinguished;
Stubborn dreams
Did witness bear
That you are there
And mine to be;
And now I face you
With my eyes cast down
Like a shy schoolboy
At exams.

I mounted siege
Well-armed with words
To storm your heart
And shatter doors;
Amazed, I stare through
Your irissed eyes,
And all forgotten
Are my darts and bow—

Forgive me love,
Chaos chokes my words.

Grant me
A breath,
A finger's touch
In 'change
For countless hours
Of yearning;
Please say
Just one kind word!

In the Mansions
Of Your Face

Your face,
My spacious home—
Close to mine,
Your sky-blue eyes,
A pillow for my soul.

When your lips,
Resting softly,
Silently cradle
My name,
All my limbs

Become lithe
And bright.

When you pledge
Our dream "to life"
With your smile—
A chalice of wine—
My ashen faith
Grows young
And green.

When,
With your smile—
That seal so sweet—
You press my fate
To your breast in love . . .

To Heaven.
A stairway
Ascends
My heart

Your face,
My spacious home—
Close to mine,
Your sky-blue eyes,
A pillow for my soul.

A Lady Pledged

Dreams,
Dear one in hope,
Promised you to
My eager longing;
I dare not cross
The borders pass-ported
Only in dreams.

How can I pay
The duties of entry
On treasures of love
At the toll of your heart?
Would you have it
In the veiled coin of pasts,
Or in the ecstatic stirrings
Of the now?

Meanwhile,
I hug the road
To ends of barely-
Guessed-for distance,
And the gospel—You exist,
Is my secret nourishment.

When you
Reveal yourself
In a gracious mood,
I barely sip an echo
Of your voice;
I treasure your
White, wide gestures,
The poor possession
Of the richest love.

My words proceed,
As the light of remote stars,
Arriving late to you;
Take note, my love,
Know this at least,
The focal-point
Of my love, my life,
Was always you.

Dedication

O pledged mine!
Heal my sadness;
Enwrap me
In a word from you;
Be a barrier

III. To a Woman in a Dream

Against my unrest,
For my ecstasy,
A platform!

My youth
And home I pawned;
My dreams
Are as yet unrealized;
They rise up
Incessantly in tides
That flow out
In the ebbs of Eternity.

I roam,
Goaded, guided,
Uncannily propelled
By nets of reins;
My tired limbs
Renew their strength
On the most narrow pallet
On which they rest.

Permit my strivings'
Boat to nest,
Upon your swelling waves;
May my visions,
Away on distant journeys
Find a haven in your sweet face.

O pledged *mine!*
Heal my sadness;
Enwrap me
In a word from you;
Be a barrier
Against my unrest,
For my ecstasy,
A platform!

In Your Arms

From the sheer
Bowl of your hand,
Let me drink
Consoling rest
In the deepest pool
Of your voice;
Let me extinguish
The searing riddles.

My fervor seared
Both cloth and skin;
I roam about
In tatters, torn,
Yet bright, and beg
A thread of silken

III. To a Woman in a Dream

Voice to nurse
The wound of
Confusion.

This world is
Veiled, invisible,
And hid behind
That other world
To come;
Thus, at least,
Like blind fingers,
Let me read
Your Braille
With my lips.

From the sheer
Bowl of your hand,
Let me drink
Consoling rest
In deepest quiet
Of your voice;
Let me extinguish
The searing riddles.

Awkward Moments

Proud silences
Stand in the hall
Distorted;
An exacerbated
Tapestry of flowers
Moves in some
Uncanny cold;
A candelabra,
Liana-like,
Gropes downward
From the ceiling.

Then your coming
Blinds my eyes

And I,
A drowning man,
Thrash about
In a sea of
Awkwardness.

Eyes to Dream

I never
Set my eyes
On yours,
Except to dream
Your face;
And now I drink
My dream's
Last dregs.

*In my whole
Lost youth,
I never said
The word of
Meeting—
"You!"
Still,
Never did I
Dare complain
At longings
Dire defeats.*

*Without your love
My sight is blind;
Give blessing*

To my presence;
Allow it here,
Help and tell me please—
"Your love must be,
So let it be."

Please lead my
Waiting
Out of deserts,
Delightful stirrings
Save my life!
I feed on
My amazement—
Grant me delight,
Lest I suffer plight.

I never
Set my eyes
On yours,
Except to dream
Your face;
And now I drink
My dream's
Last dregs.

The Longing of My Early Youth

How much
I wish to be in love,
To be close to someone
And to wander
Pleasantly in dreams,
To serenade someone
With stormy, raging songs.

How much
I wish to be in love,
To believe in
You, exclusively,
That you really are
Tender and dear, mine,
To give you all
My wondrous joys,
Worlds set to prose.

How much
I wish to be in love,
To go about
Drawing magic runes—
You, you,

My smoldering fantasy
Filled with your face,
Your whims to be
My holy creed,
Your musing smile
My consolation
From despair.

How much
I wish to be in love,
For each moment
I have prepared
A birthday gift—
I do not know, I swear—
What purchases
My longing made
In dream,
Come and take
My heart's dearest
Treasure,
My Love!

Wonder, Anticipation

Your face—
God's escutcheon;
Your arms—

III. To a Woman in a Dream

God's scepter;
Your beauty—
How well I know,
A poet's proof
Of Divinity.

Your shoulders,
Pale like the moon,
Parnassus in your eyes,
My hair, a flaming firebrand,
Cools sweetly, in the bowl of your hands.

I am a sentinel sent
To guard your mysteries.

Enthroned
In the timbre
Of your voice,
You don
A silver crown
Of brilliant
Tinkling laughter.

I am a sentinel sent
To guard your mysteries.

My life is
Star-studded

With your proud,
Quiet words.

When first
I touched—
How did I dare?
Your heavenly
Soft shoulder,
You took my
Right to wonder
And sealed it
With your name.

Ever since that day,
My ear bears echoes
Of your voice,
So dim, and yet,
Beckoning strongly;
I am by thousands
Feast days richer.

In Farthest Intimacy

Hours proceed
Hours in pilgrimage
To join Eternity,

III. To a Woman in a Dream

And my lips crouch
On the skin-hued threshold
Of your sweet,
Tall fingers;
I know I kiss
A life to come;
Your white eyes
Reflecting brightness,
Gently rocking irises,
Boats laden with dreams
From far away,
Glances revealing
Their heavy intoxication.

The hours pass,
Pilgrim-like into forever,
And your steps,
Proud and passion
Weakened,
Lead you to the broad,
Black cage
Of songbirds
Trapped in thrall.

Your fingers tease
The keyboard gently,
A flock of thin birds;
I gather pauses

*Of silence from
The secret shrine
Of yearning nights
And sparks from
Your unfettered
Intimacy.*

*So I did find out
That you, my love,
Did deign to quench
My thirst for wonder;
And I too can heal
Your last deep longing
And call your soul
My Thou.*

When you left at eventide,
I saw your tired shoulders,
Balancing lightly in equipoise,
A mystic load of haloes;
Your soul was then
My Thou.

IV.

BETWEEN ME
AND THE WORLD

Between Me
And the World

When my steps
Trod skull-like
Cobblestones
And my soles,
Like holy pilgrims,
Touched the ground,
Like hand-to-head
In-blessing,
I knew for once
That I contained
In my breast
A message
For Heaven,
And that each
Moment of my life
Was asked
By God.

My eyes,
Like prisoners
In solitary,
Looking through
The narrow bars—
How heavy did

Those sacred thongs
Weigh on my hands,
Binding their movement!

Twixt me
And the world,
Always stood,
My God
Blocking me.

Then did a
Longing rise—
I took hold of you,
The real world;
I filled my ready
Sprouting heart
With leaven
And wanted to
Tell my self
With starry eyes—
Go on!
Past thirst
And satisfaction,
On to ecstasy;
But dreams came,
Drawing out my glances,
And because
Of satisfaction

I lost the way
To that ecstasy
And can only
Wander on
To find the silent
Bridges
To my God
In my heart.

To Yehiel, Winter 1929

Youth

I came looking
For some backbone
For the unrest
Of my dream

. . .

To the
Stiff-necked
Monks
Assembled
In their
Charterhouse,
The wood,
The trees

Stand here,
A choir
Arrested amid
Procession's steps
And wait
For one who
Long ago
Promised
To appear,
To come
Here.

No cantor
Leads them;
Wordless is
Their prayer;
Yet the heart
Feels the
Tugging
Magnetic
Attraction
There.

Head
Stretched past
The heads
Before them,
Trees stand straight

And peer;
And my youth
Can wait
No longer,
Subduing
Its desire,
Demanding
This moment
Pay wait's
Hire.

I came looking
For some backbone
For the unrest
Of my dream

. . .

To lonely
Hermits
In the cities,
Rushing gaily
In the noisy roar;
On boulevards,
Trees reaching up;
Chained,
They wait
On fenced-in lots;
God! our patience

Is unending,
But our pain
Is greater,
Greater
Still.

Leafless elms
Stand between
Lampposts,
Like lampposts
Bereft of light,
And an echo
Come-from-heaven
Floods my ear,
Screaming out
The pain of all
Wounds' plight!
And my youth
Can wait
No longer,
Subduing
Its desire,
Demanding
This moment
Pay wait's
Hire.

Secrets of My Longing

Grief,
My mother,
Grays and weeps;
And I, battle weary
Of warring moods,
Wrestle with
Fatal longings
To survive—
No wonder
My grief
Sheds
Tears.

And whispers
Tenderly
And gently:
Why is it
Not enough
For you to be
A leaf in Spring's
New birth,
And drain
Each moment's
Fortune?

Dear Mother,
Don't you know?
My veins flow
With longing
'Stead of blood;
In the steep
Of waiting
I find courage,
In the last hour—
My nearest gate.

At times,
My feelings
Surge and rush,
Musing that I am
Noah's ark,
Filled with all
The longings of life,
My heart trembling
At their thirst.

Here I stand,
At that door,
About to burst
Its bolts and
Break open;
Close by,
I hear the secrets

Of my yearning,
Beating
To break it
Down.

I make
My way
Through
World
And life,
Past words,
To other words
In walking dream,
And people
Warn me
That each road
Leads to a
Flaming pyre
Of dreams.

Like a child
Weaning from
Its mother,
I feel thirst
Longing for
My God.

In the Park

A sadness
Gripped me
Like a vise
Between my
Table and chair;
I escaped
Anxiously
And ran
And found
A place for my
Weary frame,
The shoulders
Of a bench;
And there
I met the dusk
So darkly.

Thin-limbed trees
Stand in a circle
Like ascetics,
Kabbalists,
Suddenly arrested
In their ecstatic dance;
Crouching like a penitent

Awaiting the lash,
A bench stands
On its hands
And knees.

Other trees,
More simple,
Look on agape,
With windblown
Leafy shtreimels,
As if to snatch
Shirayim from it.

Some fir trees
Snore in trance
Cataleptic,
Or whisper secrets
To each other's crowns,
Past the shacks
At the outskirts
Of town,
As lonely as stone
Vaults amidst
Graves.

Humble homes,
Bewindowed—
Just big enough

To let my head through
And appear, saying,
*"Good morning
And good cheer"*—
As I stroke your
Thatched roofs tenderly
In blessing, as upon
A child's pate.

And then
A little
Mocking bird
Steps up to me,
All daring,
And gestures
A Torah trope,
An amazing glance,
Learned and insightful,
So scholar-like in challenge:
*"Man! Why do you darken
Sunshine's splendid
And rippling light
With melancholy's
Shadow?"*

A tree-dropped
Caterpillar crawls
Across my lap

To console me;
Choirs of grass
Deep in prayer,
Beg a little
Gladness for me.

Oh sadness!
Familiar,
Spent in parks
Nearby.

Lonely

Lonely—

Shut are the
Entrances to my soul.
If I could only shout
"Where are you?!"
At doors past—
But I am a stranger
To my Self.

I stand
Hours long
In dreaming-trance,

But only beside my Self,
Like some sapling
At a mountain's foot,
Wondering,
"Can I possibly grow
Beyond that peak?"

Often,
I seem to me
A ray of light
Breaking through
An unseen cleft
Into a darkened hall—
Cruel yearning
Is my eternal
Jury.

Suppressed
Primal responsibilities
Scream in rage in me—
So much fire,
So little light—
"Why do I lack fervor
In command?"
"Why did I not convert
My blood to courage?"
How bitterly I know
That I can never

Recognize my face
On me:
Why is each moment
Judged by panels
Of the present,
When each breath
Sounds the alarm
Of new futures.

Yet I pride
Myself to myself;
My intentions
Are secrets
I keep from me,
My will a mystery—
Now I want more
Than more,
Now, less
Than nothing.

Therefore,
I suffer sad
Longings for me;
Neither friends
Nor songs can
Represent my Self;
Caprice and longing
Find my riddled will;

Human — God's Ineffable Name

An altar seeking flame
Sings softly in me;
A sacrifice am I,
Or darkest danger,
And to this moment
A stormy pain,
Angrily consumed me;
From night to night
My yearning
For my Self
Grows to
Extremes.

My youth—

Pain, respite, cry,
Anger—all mine;
And despair
Casts me
To my feet
*"You are unworthy
To be You"*

Lonely—

Undefined.

My Seal

Why not a
Flower, human?

Bless me,
My disposition
With tenderness
'Stead of power!

Oh! To be
Rich in joy
'Stead of words,
To give others light
With orchid-locks,
To give them love
And delight.

And when
From room
To room I walk,
My steps climb
An arpeggio for strings—

Oh! Tenderness,
God's Secret Aura,

Be Thou my life's
Parable!

Debts

Hours demand,
They protest—

*"When will you pay on
Your dreams' debts?"*

Each hour
Bequeaths a legacy,
And days protest
As years!

Words beguiled me,
Intoxicating me
With alienation;
I am a hero
Only when I wait,
Mighty only
In my fervor.

Yet I have not yet
Repaid the world

For a single breath—

How dare I
Borrow time
To enter the
Future?

Dreams are debts,
Sonnets oaths—

When will I pay on
My dreams' debts?

When I Wander

When I wander
Through boulevards
Of poetry,
Blinding visions,
I whisper secrets
To that space
In which reside
My most raw
Mysteries.

I do not wish
To advertise
My God
On busy
Streets,
But rather
To find a
Hidden
Moment
To celebrate
The birthday
Of Eternity.

I want to
Raise up
Fields of grain
From harvests, old,
Of feeling-ferment
Word-wine for
Generations
Far ahead
In the coolest
Abysses of
A song.

Cirrus Clouds

Cirrus clouds
Stretch like
Keyboards,
And hands
Like pillars
Grow tall;
And it seems
To me
That I move
In a dream
Passing self
And world
In rooftop
Pride.

Somewhere
In this world
I live like a piano,
Am played like
Child-fingers
On Mother's
Breasts;
I know what
They say—
Human fingers

Despairing—
And still thirsty
Silence
With sounds
Of my song.

Almost,
I no longer
Need borrow
Images from eyes,
Song to make
My confessions;
Almost, I forget
The excitement
Of feeling
In the cage
Of words
Imprisoned.

V.

PANTOMIMES
OF NATURE

My Song

In silence
Transfiguring
I nursed words
In a dream,
And my eyes
Like birds
Did brood and
Hatched themselves
A vision.

And if
Some sound
Seeks passage
From me,
The winds part
Aisles to give it space;
And if some image
Tries to reach me,
Space parts a little
To let it pass.

My songs
Hang before me
Like God's
Holy Names

In some no-place
Built of holy words
Sounding organ
Preludes in my ears
And light a vigil flicker
In my heart.

Summer

Today,
Rain spread
Brandy on the fields;
Amidst the woods
A drunken tree
Yields to dancing.

Juice-sweet berries
Turn their young-blooded heads
And blades of grass revel,
And romp in their beds.

Clouds join hands
Like elves in an
Enchanted dance,
Whilst the rocky road
Reveals it road-essence,

V. Pantomimes of Nature

And reeling amidst them,
My many heady selves.

A soundless
Song in harmony
With unspent
Tears of joy
Blending with
Tender yearning
And grateful bliss;
Embracing branches
Strain toward me
And reach with their
Outstretched
Fingertips.

Field and brook come
Bearing kisses on their lips;
My breast's breath leaves
Leaves moist with dew;
Yet I am all—
A silent sunbeam
In blue ether,
Bereft of words
And breath,
Consumed
In thrall;

I am nothing,
Nothing—
Yet all!

I Befriend Woods

My tree,
My lover—
I *like* streets
And fields,
But you I *love!*
You I love still more!
You are a soul
Unrecognized
My darling,
Answering rarely
And quietly.

Barely,
In some dream,
You trees of the woods
Know me well
From the solitudes
I share with you
A love in secret;
And in the pulse

V. Pantomimes of Nature

Of some branch
I hear and understand,
And feel most clearly,
The devout gesturings
Of your mime
So mournful;
As soon as I enter
The woods,
Almost on tiptoe
I am transformed
In tree-ness
And call you sire,
My parent spruce!
Your child come to you,
Beginning to mumble
In the tongue of mutes
Telling the tree-folk
How I feel—
How well I am,
Or how sad,
And how I yearn
Long and seek;
And when some
Gust abducts a leaf
In some strange thicket
I reach out gently
And put it right,
Like a mother

With her child's hair;
Somewhere between
Wind and wall
Some tree-let,
Young and thin,
Broke an arm
Suddenly
And I tore off
My cloak and dressed it
With my sleeve as bandage.

Tammuz
In the Fields

Poplars,
Well crowned,
Green flamingoes
Hiding bills under
Feathered wings,
Stand on their
Long lissome legs
And proudly preen
Their feathered
Plumes.

V. Pantomimes of Nature

Warm earth,
An opiate for
One's feet,
Sun-baked fields,
Radiant and sweet,
Fresh and fragrant
As if they and world
Were just created.

All lie in heat
In the bosom
Of the sun
And sip the wind,
The ambrosial juice
Of space;
How good,
How pleasant
To drink this secret
And nibble contentedly
On a blade of grass.

Then subtly,
Sparse at first,
Some drizzle
Drops gently
Asperging earth
From a dust-dry curse;
A *shofar* blast

Thunders and brings
A purging shower,
Exorcising drowsy
Demons from the land.

The soul fans
Quiet joy, so lightly,
And grateful fields
Kiss the moistened toes
Of air sprites;
Gently sobered fields nurse
Renewed with purest tenderness
The Universe.

Waterfall

The river rushes,
Thrashing and breathing thunder,
As if somewhere, someone
Tore libraries of heavy
Tomes asunder.

Birds fan wings to wind
Like batons in wave-like symphonies,
Or water rushing tympanies.

On a sky blue canvas
Billow and move
Hoary charcoal sketches of leaves,
Remainders of primeval life.

The river rushes,
Thrashing and breathing thunder,
As if somewhere, someone
Tore libraries of heavy
Tomes asunder.

A Sunday
In July in Berlin

Today this city
Belongs to the trees;
Not to the Bourgeoisie,
Citizens of a proud realm;
The streets have been
Conquered by branches.

With leafy torches raised
They gather light for every eye;
They hold their plates out for sun
To serve up a virile radiance.

City no longer
Do you belong to burghers,
But to us who remain within you;
The promenading émigrés
Have left you to the loneliest
And barred your gates
With silence.

And we,
With torchlight in our eyes,
With the cold fire of solitude,
Forgotten by all others,
Love you, days forlorn.

Autumn —
Greatest Love

The trees are
Beside themselves!
Pressing their rainbow bliss,
Shamelessly shedding their garb
And pouring forth foam of limb.

The trees are
Beside themselves!
Orchards knowing no shame,

Casting all their leaves
Seductively at a lover's feet.

All the proud
Summer days
In one night turn
To lovers' lays;
Leafy crowns fall
Trickling down.
Tempting and inviting
A lover's toss.

As shards of crown
And tree flash their colors,
The lover enters his orchard lithe
And kisses as one entranced
With a feather's delicacy
And dies sumptuous deaths
Amidst the sweetest
Sorrows.

Snow on Fields

In bruised space
Stand trees stumped;
The wind saws,

Fells trees of cloud;
Like motes of sawdust
The virgin snow falls
Humbly like holy pilgrims.

My own words,
Companions,
Must crouch upon
The earth
And wean them
From their
Sightlessness,
Noises, smudges
In the air
Are erased
In soft caresses.

All the fallow
Flaws of field
To be covered
With velvet fleece;
But soiling soles do
Quash the snow
And lachrymose
It runs wet;
The trees want
To shrivel
To mere stumps

Until again
The wind saws
Clouds.

Sea

Learn from forest
To be silent,
From stars
To God to meet!
You thunderous riddle,
Is there no answer
In your surf?

Waves
Come weeping,
Come sobbing,
Like children who
Cry, cough and sputter—
"Oh what? What's that?
What? What?"
My children—
God's children!

Who can live
By the law of sea,
Ever swelling,

Never rising,
And Know not
A holiday
Nor death?

A gigantic captive
Heaves there;
Heavy fears,
Waves of sweat

Result from the
Effort to be free.

Billows urge
And fight like heroes
To pave the way
For bubbling foam
To carry them
To shore.

Every drop
Wailed forth its cry
Arousing all
To a final pity—
What does your
Screaming
Ask of me?

V. Pantomimes of Nature

The waves lament—
*"Why was might
Given me?
Why was I roused?
Why was I created?
Tell me whose
Thirst I am to still?"*

Suns sing,
Stars shine,
Waves weep,
And always did,
Telling us who
And why we are!

Who are you
If not the pain
Of tears?
For the whole
Wide world of years
Heaven glides by
And in whisper says,
*"Lament go on
For you and me!"*

My ear is cleansed
And bright my hearing;

In a single tear
I am immersed;
And I sanctify
Myself and bless:
"Silent waves!
Give ear, O sea,
A person speaks
To you!"

I know a port
For urging waves,
Which in broad words,
Waits loyally,
And will reveal
This secret—
God!

Dusk

A last thrilling
Throb of yearning,
Alone the grass,
And God addresses
No one, *"Be,"*
But, *"Hush."*

V. Pantomimes of Nature

Shrouded clouds,
Like sentinels,
Accompany
The demise of
A sinking sun
With endless quiet,
Disconsolate.

Ruefully,
Bent over pails,
They empty udders
While eyes blink
The gloomy troth
Of night in
Mourning,
As if bereft
Of mother's
Love.

At barriers long
And longed for,
Thirst dry
And dreaming,
A girl finds
The hidden face
Of her lover—
One not yet
Granted

Human — God's Ineffable Name

By desire
Alone.

Holy demands in hand,
The resurrected hour
Has come and reflected
From silvered-purple
Pregnant rivers
Swirled to their brims
With lust.

When sad,
Soft tears
Bedew the field
With their longing,
While the city sky
Reflects a glow
Of rush in
Weeping
Song.

With heady stillness
Flows this hour,
As trees work
Their magic,
Centering down
To occult
Night.

Here and there
Some footsteps
Play sad nocturnes
On a sidewalk;
With heady stillness
Flows this hour.

At Night

Night shuttered
The window
On the horizoned
Expanse of sea.

The wind reels
And causes to roil;
Long white
Tallow candles,
The whipped crests
Of white caps.

A star's
Flaming trajectory
Arcs downward;
Soon arms all over
Will stretch forth,

Blazes in hand,
And march in procession.

Flames,
Serrated and hot,
Crowning gigantic trunks
From the shores
Of the sea
To the edge
Of the world
Open the gates
Of infinities
Not ours.

The waves roll on
And push behind
The crests;
Above them
Gulls play catch
With wings,
Tossed free
As the last flame
Is extinguished.

Earth

People ask me
What I own;
Here's my answer—
"Field and dew."

My wife, she does
Lament each night
"The bread! It's riddled
With bran."

Be still!
The last complaint
You left behind in the store,
Now your trust in the field.

Our land,
She wears a beard,
All full with grain on stalks.

From mirror honed
Curve of the scythe
There drips the juice
Of grass, rich like jam.

Human — God's Ineffable Name

I am a well of
Sweat and eagerness
And earth will
Bread itself for me
Like ice that waters
Itself softly.

Effort and will,
These are my worth,
My dowry,
Wedding gift
To Earth.

I fathered
Every fruit and root
And you Earth are
Mother of our brood.

VI.

TIKKUNIM*

---

* In Kabbalah, *tikkunim* refers to the means of atonement, to reparations, to setting things right and fixing the world; it calls to mind the phrase, "to establish the Kingdom of the Almighty on Earth."

Guilt

When at times
I hear doors
In darkness
Creaking,
Innocent criminals
Seeking despair,
My heart drags heavier
With their steps
And throbs
In bitter agonies;
Would that I
Were a dog
Leading home
As seeing eye
The lost in life.

And when with
Murder blade in fist
The winos swear
To murder their
Nocturnal friends
Of dreams,
And on their
Killing paths
Do sob:

"God forgive me!"
I vomit the last
Drop of hoarded joy,
And my dreams
Take their own life
In despair.

You blessed me
God, with guilt,
Solid and immense—
Could I be most
Guilty of my peers?
Still torture me
The consolations;
I, who am most entangled,
In all the Gordian knots
Tied of twine
Of world and God—
"All guilty are, else none."

How long
Will you continue
To assure me,
Conscience dark, yet light,
Of innocence
I can't accept?

Forgiveness

I worry
When I wash
And think—
"Water is the
Laborer's sweat
Of millions.

Bag-ladies are
My homeless sisters;
I live my own
Past lives
In sinister
Criminals.

Of everyone
Murdered,
I think I
Was their killer's
Accomplice.

That I myself
Do bear the blame
For causing the shame
Of my neighbor.

Unawares, in me,
My self confesses,
"Thousand-fold—
I caused your hurt."

I want to cast
My head at doorsteps
Of jails and hospitals
And beg your pardon.

The Shlimmazel

A laid-off laborer
Sits on a stair
Of someone else's porch
And thinks . . .
Night again, dark and cold
No job, no home,
Just bleak despair.

When mother screamed—
"You pest! You glutton's maw!
You fodder fiend!"
So I slept on the earthen floor
And sang of exotic dancers.

Served a doctor as lackey—
So the chauffeur said I'm a leper,
And the maid she said I had V.D.,
And eczema from head to toe.

So here I sit and think, sadly:
Someone must be right
In cold and night;
But Listen God!
Mother please!
I feel so bad!

In God believes
No one save God;
Real people love
Themselves alone;
It's beasts who take
That life they own
And all despise the
Humble pardon.

Is a Song of this Sort For Singing?

Is a song
Of this sort
For singing?

Millions work
In mines,
Their lungs corroded,
Suffering;
No one turns
To prayer,
The mauler
Is adored;
One decrees
Another's death;
Murderers
Shed blood,
And children
Suffer pangs.

Is a song
Of this sort
For singing?

God! How sad
And cruel it is!
Generations went
Ahead of us,
Sowed confusion
To line the roads
So that we
No longer know

What's good,
What's right.

Gentle Friend

Don't you know
Stock exchanges
Are the courts of
Last resort?
That people's values,
Aims and feelings
Are judged in dollars
Like some tort.

Millions read
The marqueed lines
Of Hollywood's
Clever scripture;
But none know
Longing's secret urge;
For the thirsty,
There's only
One's own
Blood.

Come with me
Away from here
Where battle reigns
In the realm of words,
Where the most honest
Are turned into
Hateful tyrants
While seeking
To save a world

Come, please,
Come away with me!

No! I'll stay
With my generation.

At Night

A bird,
Lost in loving
Reverie,
Presses its body
To a tree's
Young trunk;
Some orphaned pup

VI. Tikkunim

Chokes and yelps
Under a musty beam.

Somewhere
In bottomless
Space, alone,
A sick star
Breathes its last;
Stones whisper
Hoarsely
In their sleep
And beg for tears
To weep clean
Their need.

I feel the
Wounded hearts
Of women weak
And shamed;
My ears seek out
The hidden sighs
To share another's
Deepest pain.

Wherever
There is one
Who weeps
Our tears,

They are
Our own;
Wherever worm
Writhes in pain,
The pain is ours.

Prayer for all Rulers

Lord of Hosts,
Do not bestow
On me the shame
Of vict'ry and might;
If my debasement
Will console my victims,
Then defame me!

My soul seethes
In stubborn refusal—
"Anything for me, but combat!"
If ever I take up arms
To wage war,
I beg you to
Defeat me!

My heart will bear
With greater ease

VI. *Tikkunim*

The pain of losing and defeat
Than victory's intoxication.

Those whom justice
Has betrayed,
Help and protect them;
I would rather
Be the wronged
Than puffed-up
With triumph
And pomp!

Proud trophies
Remind me in my joy
Of shameful deeds;
Hearts betrayed
And unmet needs.

Lord of Hosts,
Do not bestow
On me the shame
Of vict'ry and might;
If my debasement
Will console my victims,
Then defame me!

The Patient

I

In his bed
The patient sinks
Amidst others
Filled with life,
Like a gasping fish
On the shore
Of an island,
Washed up by
The waves of
The sea.

Silent pointers,
Dials racing as if
Driven by a whip;
The old familiar
Timepiece wonders,
"Which one of the fates
Will win?"

In the vise grip
Of vicissitudes,
Mute, the patient lies;
His lips parted

And supplicating:
A wife and friends
Stand around him,
And he is the loneliest
Of them all.

The dying man's heart
Hangs by some thread,
Some spider's web,
Magnetic and sweet;
The last foothold
In the hopeful corner
Shrinks and gets smaller
Beat by beat.

Past the armor,
Arms of mother
Life runs out
Through a sieve,
While the eyes
Of on-looking kin
Turn to staring stupidly
And whispering curses.

Words and mem'ries
Wiped from a skull;
Only one brief word
Remains, lost—

In the struggle
Of death's rattle,
Caught and fettered
On a vocal chord—
God!

II

Whose prayer
Will God grant?
The silent sigh,
The patient heaves,
Or raging screams
Of billions gorged full
With the patient's
Blood?

Who is Real?

Who is real,
God or I?
Let it be clear,
Ecstasy or mockery.
Somewhere
A prophet screams,
"Lord—accept our shunning!"

VI. Tikkunim

A frustrated youth shouts,
"God—you are impotent!"

Like kindling a thirst
For sparks at sight of fire,
My eyes weep to You God,
For tearing Yourself apart in world;
Let us see how Your face
Is reflected in the pupils
Of our eyes.

I swear
Each sunset
To reflect,
My heart never
To seal shut,
My eyes never
To close.

Prayer

Answer, O Lord,
Our never-ending
Yearning!
Break Your
Vaunted silence,

Cosmic King!
Release at last
The prisoners
From ages past
Who begged You
To reveal Yourself;
Leave us not
Imprisoned
In the maze;
Reveal to us
Your goodness,
Not Your cleverness;
Enthrall us not,
But teach us joy.

Why do You
Abuse our trust?
And mock us
In our pride for You?
Is our cry too great
For You to bear?
See! How we cloak
Our longing
In human passion,
Our thirst for You
In lustful acts,
While Your

VI. Tikkunim

Enduring silence
Is Hell on Earth.

Yet I can feel
Your ear
Close to my lips;
And know that
Even Your caprice
Is gentler than my
Greatest pity;
But at times,
My gall bursts, brutalized,
And with a thousand
Others screams—
"God, and God alone,
Is our adversary!"

Then, to You,
My voiceless word
I cannot speak;
And stronger
Than my faith
Is my despair;
Lord, I would gladly
Exchange holy graces,
The spiritual rungs you grant
For just one light-filled
Word from You.

Midnight Lament

At midnight,
The *Shekhinah*
Weeps and mourns,
Sitting on the lonely
Stoop of heaven;
At Her feet
A young man's
Prayer shivers—
"God—Father,
Grant me death!"

And through
The smoke of
Sacrificial ruin,
On altars of
Catastrophe,
A dying man lifts
His fist and croaks—
"Cosmic Usurer,
Be cursed!"
And even God
Blasphemes divinity
When heavenward
A forest of dense,

Naked hands,
Reach for help
In prayer protest
And plead in night.

Sunshine,
Blood of eventides
You didn't console,
Did not redeem;
And God beating
The divine breast
In infinite remorse
Pleads—
"Why am I so
Ashamed to
Show mercy"?

Teshuvah

All the pleas
Of generations—
Did they reach You?
Did You hear?
Life oblations,
Fervent deeds of love—

Did these not tell You
Of our love?

God! In Your silent
Mighty secret
You Respond
With riddles
To our call;
Are You not
The One who
Harbors bandits?
Why don't You
Bring on hatred's fall?

Yet, at times,
A tear drops gently—
"'It's Your own
Sorrow for a world"
And I feel how
Saddened, bashful
You are, God,
For Self and for us.

Still our pain
Demands Your mercy;
Not Your tears,
But Your help;
May each person's hope

VI. Tikkunim

Be Your directive,
An every shudder
Sound an alarm.

Let us all, dogs,
People and God,
Atone together
And return,
Or do penance
For one another;
Forgive us, God
For the sins we sinned,
And we will forgive You
Of Yours.

Why can't God say,
"I am sorry?"

At night,
The *Shekhinah* grieves
In Her *shiv'ah*
At the lonely gates
Of Heaven.

My Song

O World!
I want to offer you
My limbs as ligatures,
My words, my hands,
The wonder of my eyes.

Draw me into
Serving You
And return me
To Your good;
Set me down
On pedestals
In lonely railroad
Waiting rooms,
A greeting statue
Welcoming the lonely
Host-less guests,
To be throat-full
With joyous words,
Cheering them.

Send me to
My exiled kin
Languishing

VI. Tikkunim

Behind bars;
Send me,
With good news,
To console
The bereaved,
With help to
The destitute,
To heal the sick.

Take me, World,
As a friend;
Take me as
Your servant.

Appendix:
Two Poems

The first of the following two poems was written by me after Heschel suffered a heart-attack in 1969 and was accompanied by the first translations I sent to him. The second was written after his passing in 1973 and was included in the privately printed edition of these poems I made that same year.

— Z.M.S-S.

On Wellgetting

For A. J. Heschel

Why scare us
Awesome pulsebeat,
God's knock,
With not beating
Again?

Even a scare
Needs you
To beat,
But quietly
And gently—
The brain thirsts
For food.

Each pain's
Explosion
Retaliated
With a white bomb
Of nitroglycerine—
Why bother then?

Lord, make peace,
Give breath and rest
Sleep and a calm,

So that with
Each heartbeat,
One may acknowledge You,
And know You again
In heartbeat of love,
Dream and fervor;
Open the gate—
Come and breathe me,
But I beg You,
Don't upset me.

Z.M.S-S.

In Memoriam,
Rabbi Abraham Joshua Heschel

So you left us,
Teacher and friend;
Finished Kotzk
And left abruptly;
You lived with
Jacob-Israel, our sire,
And left with him,
And left us blessed
With the fruit

Of heart and mind,
Soul and strength.

You sure did pick
A difficult time
In which to bring
The Why of
Being a Jew to us—
But only you could help
When there were none
Who could enunciate
The paradox:
"Live- by thy blood"
And drenched in it.

No other has
So eloquently said
That the ineffable
Is just that . . .
And yet the glimpses
You showed us
Of the light and time
Which uttered by Eternity
Shaped our destiny as Jews—
Though not in Space.

And "Who is Man?"
You wrote and spoke,

Human — God's Ineffable Name

Yet louder than your word,
Your work for peace,
Truth and kindness,
Here and now;
You Abraham
Were Vietnamese,
A Priest, our man in Rome,
Jerusalem, New York,
At JTS you were the Mentsch
Protecting objectors.

Your sire was known
As Israel's lover;
You will not be known
As less than he;
Your love
For all humanity
Will be with us
Who see you still
With rage prophetic,
Urging deeds,
With smile encouraging
Sabbath's bliss.

Z.M.S-S.

Biographies

Abraham Joshua Heschel (1907-1972) was one of the most celebrated and original Jewish thinkers of the twentieth century. Though renowned in his day as a theologian and philosopher, Heschel is also celebrated today for his tireless activism against the war in Vietnam and his work for civil rights with Dr. Martin Luther King Jr. He is the author of numerous spiritual classics, including: *The Prophets, The Sabbath, Man is Not Alone, God in Search of Man,* and *The Earth is the Lord's.*

Zalman M. Schachter-Shalomi (b. 1924) is the father of the widely influential Jewish renewal movement and one of the most important spiritual leaders in the world today. He is the author of such acclaimed works as *Jewish with Feeling, Spiritual Intimacy,* and two authoritative works on Hasidism, *A Heart Afire* and *A Hidden Light.*